C000006380

rainbow

2000

rainbow 2000

Pupil's Book 4

Sandra Slater

Adapted by Michael Thornton

MACMILLAN

© Copyright text Sandra Slater 1989
© Copyright illustrations Macmillan Education Ltd 1989
© Copyright adaptations for British English edition Macmillan
Education Ltd 1990
© Copyright adaptations for this edition Macmillan Education Ltd
1991

All rights reserved. No reproduction, copy or transmission of this
publication may be made without written permission.

No paragraph of this publication may be reproduced, copied or
transmitted save with written permission or in accordance with the
provisions of the Copyright, Designs and Patents Act 1988, or
under the terms of any licence permitting limited copying issued
by the Copyright Licensing Agency, 90 Tottenham Court Road,
London W1P 9HE.

Any person who does any unauthorised act in relation to this
publication may be liable to criminal prosecution and civil claims
for damages.

First published 1999
British English edition first published 1990
This edition first published 1991 by
MACMILLAN EDUCATION LTD
London and Oxford
Companies and representatives throughout the world

ISBN 0–333–65143–X

12   11   10   9   8
06   05   04   03   02   01

This book is printed on paper suitable for recycling and made
from fully managed and sustained forest sources.

Printed in Egypt by Sahara Printing Co.

Designed by Typematter Graphics, Basingstoke

Cover illustration by Terry Burton

Contents

Meet Magda and Alex.

Hello. I'm Alex Best. I'm ten and a half.
I'm 155 centimetres tall and I don't know how much I weigh.
I live in a house on Old Road.
I go to the New English School, in Park Road.

Hello. I'm Magda Martin. I'm eleven.
I'm 150 centimetres tall and I weigh 38 kilos.
I live in a flat near the cinema.
I go to the International School, near the bank.

Ask and answer.

Ask questions about the girl. Ask questions about the boy.

What's the girl's name?   How old is she?
How tall is Alex?   How much does he weigh?
Does Magda live in a house   Where is it?
or a flat?
Which school does Alex go to?   Where is it?

The birthday present

Point and say.

Where is she going?
What time will her flight leave?

She's going to Brunei.
It will leave at half-past seven.

He never brushes his teeth.

How often do you brush your teeth?

Name	Sat.	Sun.	Mon.	Tues.	Wed.	Thurs.	Fri.
Magda	✓✓	✓✓	✓	✓✓	✓	✓	✓✓
Alex	✓✓	✓✓	✓✓	✓✓	✓✓	✓✓	✓✓
Adam	✓	✓	✓✓	✓	✓		✓✓
Susie		✓		✓		✓	
Sam							
You							

Whose teeth are these?

These are Alex's teeth.
He has very good teeth.
He brushes them every day.
He always brushes his teeth.

Magda usually brushes her teeth.

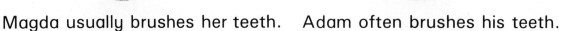

Adam often brushes his teeth.

Susie sometimes brushes her teeth.

Sam never brushes his teeth.

I always get up at half past six.

I run happily to the bathroom and have a shower.

I sometimes go to school on the bus.

I sometimes walk to school.

I usually help my mother. I never drop the plates.

I always go to bed at eight o'clock.

What's the weather like in Britain?

	SPRING	SUMMER	AUTUMN	WINTER
	March April May	June July August	September October November	December January February
Does it rain?	Always.	Sometimes.	Often.	Usually.
It is hot or cold? Is it warm or cool?	Usually warm and sunny but sometimes cool.	Usually hot and sunny.	Sometimes warm, but usually cool.	Sometimes sunny, but always cold.
Is it windy?	Usually.	Sometimes.	Often.	Often.
Does it snow?	Sometimes.	Never.	Sometimes.	Often.

Ask and answer.

Does it rain in the spring?　　　Yes, it always rains in the spring.
Does it snow in the summer?　　No, it never snows in the summer.

A song

9

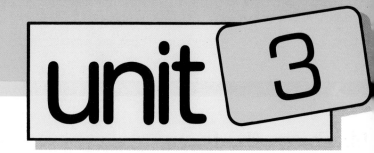

Shopping

Mrs Green and William are in the market. They are doing the shopping. They usually go to the market on Thursdays.

Mrs Green buys fruit and vegetables. She sometimes buys William ice cream.

Good morning.

Good morning, Mrs Green. What would you like today?

A kilo of potatoes and half a kilo of carrots, please.

Here you are.

Oh, and a kilo of apples, please. That's all. Thank you.

Two pounds eighty, please.

Here you are.

Thank you. Goodbye.

Goodbye.

How much do they cost?

 50p

a carton of milk

 85p

a bottle of lemonade

 90p

a kilo of apples

 45p

a can of cola

 £1.05

a packet of soap powder

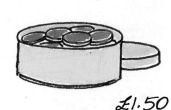 £1.50

a box of biscuits

 £1.75

a box of chocolates

 £1.10

a packet of corn flakes

 £1.10

a tin of sardines

Ask and answer.

How much does a packet of corn flakes cost?

One pound, ten.

How much does a packet of soap powder and a kilo of apples cost?

One pound five, and ninety pence . . . That's one pound, ninety five.

11

What kind of sweets would you like?

13

Who lives in this block?

Dr Nasreddin	The top floor. / The ninth floor.
Mr and Mrs Martin	The eighth floor.
Miss Green, Miss Smith	The seventh floor.
Mr Macdonald	The sixth floor.
Mr and Mrs Best	The fifth floor.
Mr Selim	The fourth floor.
Mr and Mrs Hill	The third floor.
Miss Parker	The second floor.
Mr and Mrs Bird	The first floor.
Mr and Mrs Smart	The ground floor.
The caretaker	The basement.

Ask and answer.

Who lives on the fourth floor?   Mr Selim.
Who lives in the basement?   The caretaker.
Where does Mr Macdonald live?   On the sixth floor.
Where do Mr and Mrs Smart live?   On the ground floor.

14

When's your birthday, Sonia?
It's on February the fourteenth.

When's your birthday, Sonia?

It's on February the fourteenth.

REMEMBER THESE BIRTHDAYS!!

Jan. 11th – Mum	June 21st – Grandma
Feb. 12th – Alex	July 23rd – Dad
Feb. 14th – ME!	Aug. 30th – Karim
May 18th – Tom	Dec. 31st – Magda

When's your birthday?   Can you see it here?

	January		1st, 2nd, 3rd, 4th, 5th,
	February		6th, 7th, 8th, 9th, 10th,
	March		eleventh, twelfth, thirteenth,
	April		fourteenth, fifteenth,
	May		sixteenth, seventeenth,
It's on	June	the	eighteenth, nineteenth,
	July		twentieth, twenty-first,
	August		twenty-second, twenty-third,
	September		twenty-fourth, twenty-fifth,
	October		twenty-sixth, twenty-seventh,
	November		twenty-eighth, twenty-ninth,
	December		thirtieth, thirty-first.

15

A game

What's different?

Look at the pictures of the classroom yesterday and today.
Ten things are different. Can you see them?

Yesterday   **Today**

Yesterday the books were on the floor. Now they are on the shelf.
Yesterday the ball was on the floor. Now it's in the cupboard.
Yesterday was Monday. Today is . .

What's the weather like in Sudan?

Good morning. Today I'm in Khartoum, Sudan, in Africa. It's very hot here. It's hotter than England.

Good morning. What's the weather like in Khartoum? Is it always hot here?

Yes, it's always hot!

Do you have spring, summer, autumn and winter?

No, we don't. It is hot almost all year.

Does it rain?

When? Yes.

It always rains from August to November and sometimes in December and January.

Children from different countries

I live in Australia.
I'm Australian.

I live in Finland.
I'm Finnish.

I live in England.
I'm English.

I live in Canada.
I'm Canadian.

I live in Sudan.
I'm Sudanese.

I live in Malaysia.
I'm Malaysian.

Ask and answer.

What is the Australian boy wearing?	Shorts.
Why?	Because it's very hot in Australia.
Is it always hot in Australia?	Sometimes it snows.
What is the English girl wearing?	A scarf, a coat, boots, gloves, a hat.
Why?	Because . . .

What kind of shop is it?
What can you buy there?

a bookshop

a clothes shop

a camera shop

a toy shop

a music shop

a shoe shop

Point and ask.

What kind of shop is this?   A camera shop.
What can you buy there?   Cameras and film.

22

Ask questions about the other shops, too.

Who is the oldest?
Which is the cheapest?
Point and say.

This man is old; this man is older, but this man is the oldest.

This bag is cheap; this bag is cheaper, but this bag is the cheapest.

long
longer
the longest

fat
fatter
the fattest

thin
thinner
the thinnest

Ask.

Which man is the oldest?
Which boy is the fattest?

Point and say.

This one.
This one.

The best circus in the world!

SMITH'S CIRCUS

The best circus in the world will be in your town on May the twenty-first and May the twenty-second.

> Come to the circus. Come and have fun!
> Come to the circus. Come, everyone!

> Come and see our amazing people!
> The biggest hands in the world!
> The oldest man in the world!
> The fattest man in the world!

> The tallest man in the world!
> The strongest man in the world!
> The longest nose in the world!
> The longest feet in the world!

Ask.

Which is the tallest man in the world?
Which are the longest feet in the word?

Point and say.

He's here.
They're here.

Was it true?
Was he the tallest man in the world?

I went to the circus yesterday.

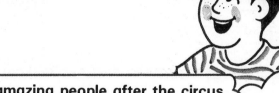

Did you? Were they amazing people?
Was he the fattest man in the world?
Were they the biggest hands in the world?
Did the thin man have the longest nose in the world?
Was it the best circus in the world?

No, it wasn't. I saw the amazing people after the circus.
It wasn't true. It was the worst circus in the world.
The fat man wasn't the fattest man in the world.

Ask and answer.

How about the strong man?

No, he wasn't the strongest man in the world.

How about the big hands?

No, they weren't the biggest hands in the world.

25

At the supermarket

1 Point and ask.

Do you like plums?

Answer.

Yes, I do.
No, I don't.

2 Ask and point.

Which do you like best?
Plums, pears or bananas?
Spinach, beans or carrots?

Answer.

Plums.
Carrots.

26

3 Ask.

Are there any plums in the picture?
Are there any courgettes?
Are there any packets of cereal?

Answer and point.

Yes, there are some plums.
They're here.
No, there aren't any courgettes.
Well, there's one packet.

Ask about . . . chops, bottles of orange juice, beans, watermelons, bags of sugar, pears, cakes, carrots, cartons of apple juice, biscuits, tins, peaches.

27

I'd like to buy some meat.
Which shop should I go to?

What are these? Point and say.

a chicken

a loaf of bread

some sugar

a tennis racquet

some medicine

a butcher's

a baker's

a chemist's

a sports shop

a grocer's

Ask and answer.

I'd like to buy a chicken.
Which shop should I go to?

You should go to a butcher's.

A game
Is anybody here?

What can you see?

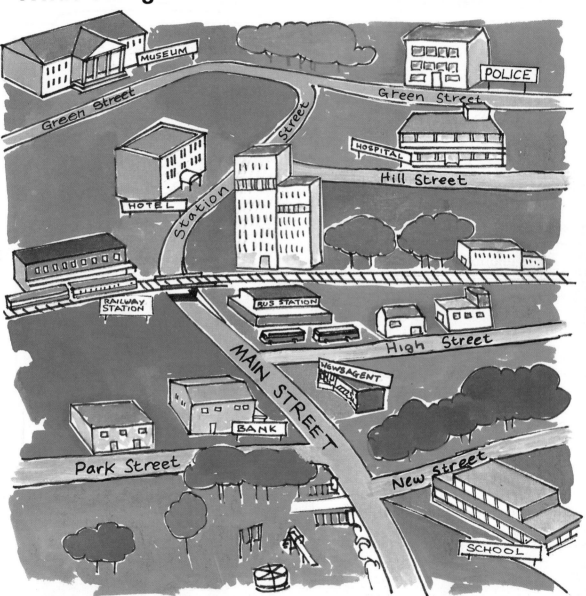

Ask and answer.

Is there a museum near the school?   No, there isn't.

Is there a museum in town?   Yes, there is.

Where is it?   It's in Green Street.

Is there a hospital in town?   Yes, there is.

Dinosaurs are more interesting than football.

Open Day at School
We will have our Open Day on Thursday,
May 15th, at ten o'clock.
Every class in the school must have
an exhibition in their classroom.

Class 4A made an exhibition about dinosaurs. This is their exhibition.

Dinosaurs lived a very long time ago.
There were no people in the world then.

(1) Brontosaurus

(2) Pteranodon

(3) Diplodocus

(4) Saltopus

Brontosaurus was the biggest and Saltopus was the smallest
Diplodocus was the longest and Pteranodon was the fastest.

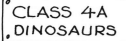

CLASS 4A
DINOSAURS

This is Tyrannosaurus Rex . (5)

It was five and half *metres* tall
and fifteen *metres* long. It had
big teeth. They were 18cms long.
It ate other animals.

This is Gallimus .(6)

It was the fastest on land
It ran as fast as a horse .

This is Torosaurus. (7) Its head was
bigger than a car.

33

That's all right.
It doesn't matter.

Hello.

No, this is Mrs Hill.

No, this is 453-8637.

That's all right.
It doesn't matter. Goodbye.

Hello. Is that Mrs Brown?

Is this 453-8636?

Oh, I'm very sorry.
I've got the wrong number.

Goodbye.

Mrs Hill

Dina

What did Tom do before he came to school?

got up

had a bath

the water was too cold!
had a shower

washed his hair

got dressed

combed his hair

ate his breakfast

brushed his teeth

helped his Mum

What did you do before you came to school today?

Ask and answer.

Did you . . .   brush your teeth? have a bath?   Yes, I did.
                 wash your hands and face?   No, I didn't.
                 have a shower? cook breakfast?
                 eat breakfast? comb your hair?
                 help your Mum? clean your shoes?
                 make a cup of coffee? wash your hair?

35

The thirteenth of June was a bad day!

It was the thirteenth of June yesterday. Tom had a bad day.

He had a hole in his sock.

He fell over the cat.

He got toothpaste on his T-shirt.

He dropped a cup.

He fell off his bicycle.

He cut his finger.

He lost his football.

I hate cats, toothpaste, bikes and football!

The story of the Three Blindfolded Men.

This story is about three men. Their names were John, Tom and David. John was the shortest. Tom was the oldest. David was the tallest. One day they played a game. They all put blindfolds over their eyes.

Then, the three blindfolded men went to the market. They walked on the path. There was something in the middle of the path. They walked into it.

"What's this?" they asked. "What's this in the middle of the path? We can't see it. What can it be?"

"Well, we can't see it, but we can touch it," said John. "Then we can guess. I'm going to touch it. I'm going to guess."

WHAT WAS IT? You can read the end in another lesson.

unit 10

Now you can read the end of the story.

He touched it. "Hmmmmm," he said. Then he guessed. "It's big and it's thick. It's a tree. It must be a tree."

Then David touched it. "Hmmmmm," he said. "No, it's not a tree. It's long and it's thin."

Then he guessed. "It's a snake. It must be a snake."

Then Tom touched it. "Hmmmmm," he said, and then he guessed. "This isn't a tree or a snake," he said. "This is a house. It must be a house."

"You're wrong! It's a tree!" shouted John.
"You're wrong! It's a snake!" shouted David.

Then a woman came.

"Please help us," they said.
"We can't see. What's this in
the middle of the path?"

John touched it again. "Is it a
tree?" he asked.

"No," said the woman. "That's
not a tree, it's a leg."

David touched it again. "Is it a
snake?" he asked.

"No," said the woman. "That's
not a snake, it's a trunk."

Tom touched it again. "Is it a
house?" he asked.

"No," said the woman. "That's
not a house, it's a body. This is
an animal. It's a big, grey
animal. It's . . .".

What is it? Can you see? Did
you guess?

39

Who is the strongest?

Don't do this! Don't do that!

Don't touch that, Alex!

Don't ride that bicycle, Alex!

Don't play football in the house, Alex!

Stop that noise, Alex!

"Don't do this" and "Don't do that". Well, I'll be good. I'll go and read a book.

Don't eat the biscuits, Alex!

Don't put it there, Alex!

Where's the shoe shop?

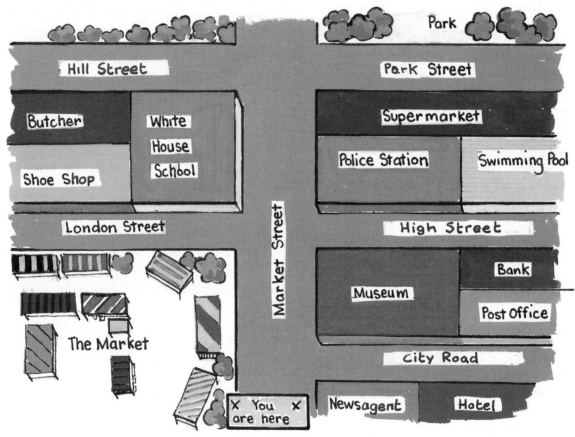

Ask and answer.

| Where's the shoe shop? | It's in London Street. It's the first street on the left. |

| Where's the bank? | It's in High Street. It's the second street on the right. |

| Where's the . . .? | It's in . . . Street. It's the . . . street on the . . . |

I want to go to the Art Museum.

Mrs Hart likes painting and drawing. She wants to see the paintings and drawings in the museum.

She wants to go to the museum, but she doesn't know where it is. She asks a girl and a policeman. She is very polite. She says ''Please'', and ''Thank you very much''.

They want to go to Istanbul.
How can they go?

TRAV

Good morning.
We want to go to Istanbul.
How can we go
and how much will it cost?

Well, you can go by bus.
That costs sixty dollars.

ISTANBUL
TRAVEL BY
BUS

Or you can go by boat.
That costs eighty dollars,
and it's slower than the bus.

ISTANBUL
BOAT

You can go by train.
That costs a hundred dolla

NBUL NEW YORK
TRAIN

You can go by plane.
That's the quickest,
but it's the most expensive.
That costs two hundred dollars.
Which would you like?

FLY

Thank you very much.
We'll go by bicycle!

The Teacher's Song

''Where's your pencil?
Where's your book?
You must listen!
You must look!''

''Be quiet, please!
Say after me!
Look through the window!
What can you see?''

Our teacher is always right.
He's never wrong!

''You shouldn't talk!
Don't make a noise!
You mustn't shout!
Be quiet, boys!''

''Pay attention!''
All day long.
''Do this! Do that!''
Teacher's never wrong!

We are always good children.

45

Parts of the body.

Do this. It's easy.

Put your hands above your head.
Clap them one, two, three.
Now put them on your hips,
Then slowly touch one knee.

Move your fingers, then your thumbs.
Lift both knees up and down.
Put both hands around your waist,
Then quickly turn around.

Put your fingers on your shoulders,
Then bend down to touch your toes.
With both your hands behind your neck,
Try to touch your ears and nose!

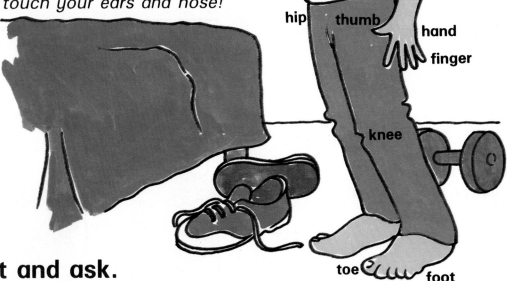

Point and ask.

What's this in English?
Can you spell it?
No, that's wrong. It should be
s—t—o—m—a—c—h.

It's a stomach.
s—t—o—m—a—k.

What's wrong?
All the children are ill today.

1 Look at the pictures and read the words.

2 Point, ask and answer.

What's wrong with Sonia?

What's wrong with Jane?

What's wrong with . . .?

She has earache.

She has a cough.

She has . . .

Sonia has earache.

Alice has stomach-ache.

Mona has toothache.

Leila has toothache.

Jane has a cough.

Diana has earache.

Nadia has a headache.

Magda has a cough.

Susanna has a cold.

47

Would you like to come to my birthday party?

I'm sorry, I can't. I have to . . .

Hello. This is Magda. Would you like to come to my house tomorrow? It's my birthday and I'm having a party.

I'd like to come, but I can't. I have to go to my grandmother's house tomorrow.

Yes, I'd like to come. Thank you very much.

I'd like to come, but I can't. I have toothache. I have to see the dentist tomorrow.

Thanks, Magda. I'd like to come, but I have a bad stomach-ache. I have to see the doctor tomorrow.

Thanks, Magda. Yes, I'd like to come.

49

I can speak a little English.

The story of Hare and Tortoise

One day, Tortoise saw Hare. She did not like Hare. Nobody liked him.

I'm the fastest animal in the world.
My legs are long and very strong.
You can't run fast. Look at your legs!
They're very short and very weak. Nobody can run as fast as me.
I'm the best!

"You're NOT the best," said Tortoise. "You're not the fastest. I'm as good as you."

"No, you're not," said Hare. "Your legs are too short. You can't run fast."

"Oh yes, I can," said Tortoise. "We can have a race. I will beat you. I will win the race." Hare laughed and laughed.

OK. We will have a race tomorrow at ten o'clock.
We will race from the big tree to the river.
But you will NEVER beat me.
I'm the best. I'm the fastest animal in the world.

Tortoise went to the big tree at five to ten. Hare wasn't there.

At ten o'clock, the animals shouted "One, two, three, go!"
Tortoise walked very slowly towards the river. Tortoises can't run.

At five to eleven, Hare came.

Hare ran quickly towards the river. Soon he was in front of
Tortoise. The sun was very hot.

Hare ate some grass and then he sat down under a tree. The sun
was very, very hot. Very slowly, Hare's eyes closed. Soon he was
asleep.

The sun was very, very hot, but Tortoise walked on and on. She did not stop. At twelve o'clock she saw Hare. He was asleep.

Tortoise walked on and on towards the river. She did not stop. She did not eat grass. She did not sleep.

At one o'clock, Hare opened his eyes. He looked behind him, but he did not see Tortoise.

Then he looked in front. There was Tortoise! She was nearly at the river.

Hare jumped up quickly. He ran very, very fast towards the river.

"Walk quickly, Tortoise!" shouted all the animals. "You can beat him!"

Hare ran fast, but he did not win the race. Tortoise beat him. She did not stop. She did not eat grass. She walked very, very slowly, but she never stopped. She won the race. All the animals were very happy, because nobody liked Hare.

Look at these pictures.
Who are these people?
Do you know them?

This is Queen Elizabeth the Second. She is Queen of England. The man is Prince Philip. He is the Queen's husband. She is his wife.

The Queen and Prince Philip have four children. They have one daughter and three sons. You can see them in the picture. Their daughter is Princess Anne. Their sons are Prince Charles, Prince Andrew and Prince Edward. Prince Charles is the oldest and Prince Edward is the youngest. Prince Andrew is older than Prince Edward, but not as old as Princess Anne.

Prince Charles' wife is called Diana. Prince Charles and his wife have two sons. Their names are Prince William and Prince Harry. Prince William is older than Prince Harry.

Look at this family tree.

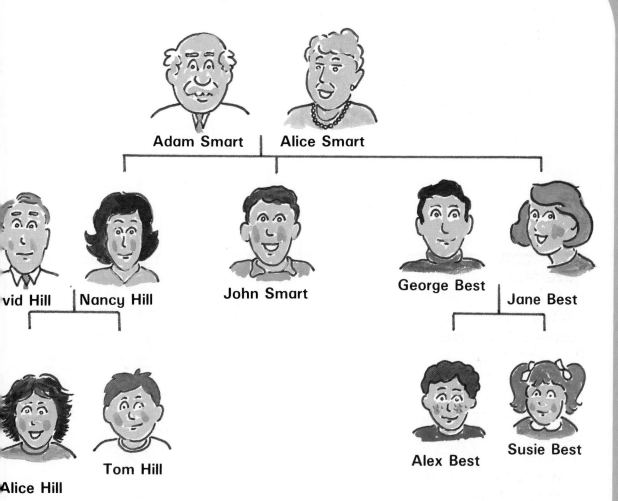

Adam Smart Alice Smart

vid Hill Nancy Hill John Smart George Best Jane Best

Alice Hill Tom Hill Alex Best Susie Best

Ask and answer.

Who is Adam Smart's wife?   Alice Smart.
Who is George Best's wife?   Jane Best.
Who is Jane Best's daughter?   Susie Best.
How many daughters do Adam and
  Alice Smart have?   Two.
How many sons do they have?   . . .
Who is Alex Best's grandfather/
  aunt/uncle, etc.?

I'm not tall enough!

Which subjects do you like?
Do you have these subjects at your school?

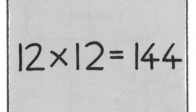
maths

science

history

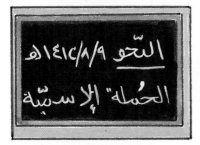
language

art

religion

English

geography

gym

Point and ask.

Do you like English?	Yes, I do.
Do you like maths?	No, I don't.
Do you like geography?	Well, it's OK.
What's your favourite subject?	Art.
What's your least favourite subject?	Science.

These are the subjects at Magda's school.

	Sunday	Monday	Tuesday	Wednesday	Thursday
8:00	Maths	Art	Maths	Science	History
9:00	French	English	History	Religion	Geography
	Break				
10:00	Religion	Geography	French	English	Maths
11:00	History	Science	Language	Maths	English
12:00	Break				
1:00	English	Maths	English	Art	Religion
2:00	Language	Religion	Gym	Geography	Gym

Ask and answer.

What's the first subject on Monday?   Art.
What's the last subject on Thursday?   Gym.
What's the third subject on Tuesday?   French.
What subject is after break on Thursday morning? . . .

59

TODAY'S TELEVISION PROGRAMMES

Morning and afternoon

Maths for Schools

One, Two, Three
(Maths for young children)

Science for Schools

News and Weather

Alexander the Great
(History for schools)

Tennis

The Pink Giraffe
(A cartoon)

Evening

Lion!
(An animal programme)

Football

Cakes and Things
(A programme about cooking)

The Avens (A soap opera)

News at Ten

Superman (A film)

The film ends.

Ask and answer.

What kind of programme is Superman?

It's a film.

What time does it start?

It starts at half past ten.

What time does it end?

It ends at twelve o'clock.

What's the second programme?

One, Two, Three.

What kind of programme is it?

It's a maths programme.

What kind of school do they go to?

61

What's your favourite job?
What would you like to be?

A doctor?

A nurse?

A flight attendant?

A vet?

A football player?

A police officer?

A pilot?

A lorry
driver?

A train driver?

A news broadcaster?

A farmer?

A carpenter?

A pop
star?

A film star?

A house painter?

A teacher?

Point, ask and answer.

What's her job?   She's a doctor.
What's his job?   He's a pop star.

A maths lesson in English

Can you read these?

$3 + 2 = 5$ $2 \times 3 = 6$

$5 + 5 = 10$ $5 \times 2 = 10$

$5 - 3 = 2$ $6 \div 3 = 2$

$7 - 4 = 3$ $6 \div 2 = 3$

Ask and answer.

$2 + 4 = ?$ 6

Two plus four is . . .?   Six

$9 - 8 = ?$

$2 \times 4 = ?$

$8 - 4 = ?$

$8 \div 2 = ?$

Some people don't like maths, but maths can be interesting.

Can you multiply by nine?
Look at this.

$1 \times 9 = 9$ $6 \times 9 = 54$

$2 \times 9 = 18$ $7 \times 9 = 63$

$3 \times 9 = 27$ $8 \times 9 = 72$

$4 \times 9 = 36$ $9 \times 9 = 81$

$5 \times 9 = 45$ $10 \times 9 = 90$

Now look again.
This is very interesting.
Look at the answers.

The first answer is nine.
The second answer is eighteen.
Eighteen is eight and one.
Eight plus one is nine.

The third answer is twenty-seven.
That's two and seven.
Two plus seven is nine, too.

The last answer is ninety.
That's nine and nought. Nine plus nought is nine

Are all the answers the same?

Some people don't like maths, but maths can be fun.

Write a number on this paper.
It must be between ten and one.
Don't show me the number.

OK.

3
3 × 2 = 6

Now multiply by two.

3
3 × 2 = 6
6 + 4 = 10

Add four.

3
3 × 2 = 6
6 + 4 = 10
10 ÷ 2 = 5

Divide by two.

3
3 × 2 = 6
6 + 4 = 10
10 ÷ 2 = 5
5 - 3 = 2

Subtract your first number.

The answer is two.

That's right!
How did you do it?
I don't understand.

Do this with your friend. Use different numbers.
The answer is always two.

What did they do yesterday?

Magda

Alex

Bobby

Mrs Green

Mrs Hill

Diana

Tom

Leila

Mr Selim

Doctor Stevens

Susie

John

Jane

Alice

Karim

Mona

ate a lot

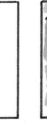
drew a picture

sat in the garden

sat in the house

bought a stamp

flew his kite

swam in the pool

wrote a letter

gave a present

rode a horse

rode a bicycle

flew to New York

went to the post box

drove his car

made a dress

made a shelf

Ask and answer.

Who flew to New York? Mr Selim.

Did Magda go to the cinema? No, she didn't. She sat in the garden.

67

Karim is writing a letter.

Karim is writing a letter.

He's putting it in an envelope.

He's writing the address on the envelope.

He's putting on a stamp.

He's taking it to the post box.

He's posting it.

At the post office

69

Leila goes to England.

PO Box 3234,
Alexandria.

January 3rd.

Dear Mona,

I have some very interesting news. I'm going to live in England.

My mother and father have new jobs in England. They are going to work at a big hospital in Manchester. I'm going to go to school there.

All my classes will be in English. It will be difficult, but it will be very interesting. Maths will be the worst subject!!!!!!

We are going to fly to England next week and I start school on Monday, January 12th at five to nine. I don't know my new address, but I will send you a postcard from Manchester.

love,
Leila

73

Where are they from?

I'm from the United States.
I'm American.

I'm from France.
I'm French.

I'm from Russia.
I'm Russian.

I'm from England.
I'm English.

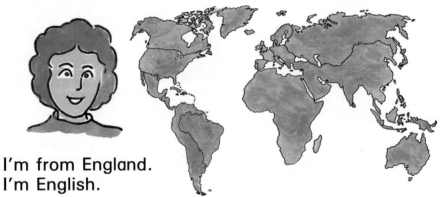

I'm from Japan.
I'm Japanese.

I'm from Egypt.
I'm Egyptian.

I'm from Pakistan.
I'm Pakistani.

I'm from Spain.
I'm Spanish.

I'm from Australia.
I'm Australian.

Point and ask.

What country is this?   Japan.
Where's she from?   Russia. She's Russian.

What is he going to do? What is he doing? What has he done?

1

What is he going to do? He's going to wash his hair.

2

What is he doing? He's washing his hair.

3

What has he done? He has washed his hair.

4

What is she going to do?
She's going to comb her hair.

5

What is she doing? She's combing her hair.

6

What has she done? She has combed her hair.

7

What is he going to do? He's going to clean the blackboard.

8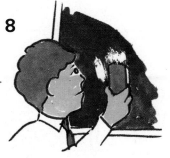

What is he doing? He's cleaning the blackboard.

9

What has he done? He has cleaned the blackboard.

Point and ask.

What is she going to do?   What is she doing?   What has she done?

Point and ask.

What is he going to do? What is he doing? What has he done?

Use these words.

open the door	wash the car	cook an omelette
run		paint a picture

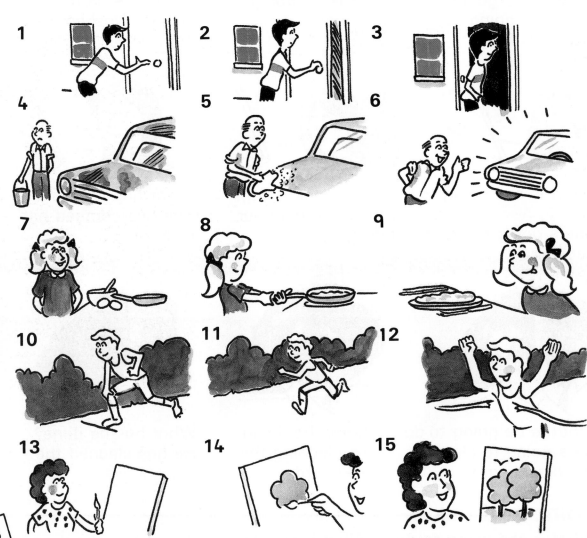

She has washed all the dishes, she has ironed all the clothes.

Look at Mum.
She's very tired.
Why is she tired?
The answer is in the poem.

She has washed all the dishes.
She has ironed all the clothes.
She has cleaned all the windows.
She has painted all the doors.

She has walked to the market.
She has made a lot of bread.
She has finished all her work.
And now she's going to bed.

I'm going to bed.
I'm very tired.

unit 20

Bobby has put on his new shirt, but he hasn't put on . . .

Bobby is going to a birthday party. He has bought a present and he has cleaned his shoes.

He has had a bath and he has washed his hair. He has washed his neck and behind his ears.

He has put on a new shirt and his best tie. He looks great.

Goodbye, Mum. I'll see you tonight.

Goodbye.

BOBBY! STOP! DON'T GO!!!!

What's wrong, Mum?

You haven't put your trousers on!

A game — What have we done?

What has he done? What hasn't he done?

Alex, I'm going to the bank.
Go to the butcher's and buy some meat.
Wash the dishes. Be careful.
Don't break the new jug.
You can eat the biscuits,
but don't eat the cake.
Don't drink the cola. You can drink milk.
Cook an omelette for your lunch.
And wash the windows.

Yes, Mum.

Ask and answer.

Has he been to the butcher's?   Yes, he has.
Has he broken the jug?   No, he hasn't
Has he eaten . . ./ drunk . . ./ bought . . ./ dropped . . ./ broken . . ./
washed . . ./ cooked . . .?

Have you ever . . .?

Read this poem.

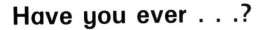

Have you ever heard a fish talk?
Have you ever seen a door walk?
Have you ever heard a horse moo?
Have you ever heard a cat count two?
Have you ever seen an elephant fly?
No, neither have I!

I've never heard a fish talk.
I've never seen a door walk.
I've never heard a horse moo.
I've never heard a cat count two.
I've never seen an elephant that flew.
Have you?

Let me in! Let me out!

Point and ask.

What is he saying?   Let me in!

There are seven days in a week.
There are twelve months in a year.
There are three hundred and sixty-five days in a year.

Ask and answer.

How many days are there in a week? Seven.
How many days are there in a year? Three hundred and sixty-five.
How many months are there in   Twenty-four.
two years?

How many days are there in   I don't know.
six years?   That's too difficult!

I've been here for two days. I've been here since Wednesday.

1 Good morning.
Today's programme is from Karachi.
I'm going to talk to people
on the street.

Good morning.
I'm from Pakistan Television.
Do you live here or are you on holiday?

I live here. I've lived in Karachi
for ten years. Am I on television? Great!
I've never been on television before!
Yes, I've lived here for ten years. I've . . .

Good morning.
I'm from Pakistan Television.
Do you live here or are you on holiday?

I'm on holiday.

Where are you from?

I'm from England.

From England! That's interesting.
How long have you been in Pakistan?

I've been here for a week.

And how long have you been
in Karachi?

I've been here for two days.
I've been here since Wednesday.

Have you ever been
to Pakistan before?

No, I've never been here before.

Do you like our country?

Yes, I like it very much.
I like your weather!
And I like the Pakistani people.

nside or outside?

> Hello, Magda.
> Would you like to go to
> the art museum this afternoon?
> About two o'clock?

> Yes, that's a good idea.
> I'll see you there.

> Hello, Nadia. What's wrong?

> What's wrong?
> I'm waiting for Magda.
> I've been here since two o'clock.
> I've been here for AN HOUR!!!!

> Have you seen her?

> No, I haven't seen her.
> I'm going inside.

> Hello, Alex. Have you seen Nadia?
> She's very late.
> I'm waiting for her.
> I've been here since two o'clock.
> I've been here for AN HOUR!!!!

> Yes, I've seen her. She's outside.
> She's waiting for you
> and she's very angry.
> She's been there since two o'clock.

> What! Outside!
> I didn't say outside!

> Where have you been?
> I've been here for an hour.
> I've been here since TWO O'CLOCK!!!!!!

85

22

In the park

Who can you see in the park? There's a woman with a red dress. There's a man with no hair. There's a boy with red shorts.

slide

swing

Ask and answer.

Who's taking a photograph?
Who's posting a letter?
Who's drinking a can of cola?
Who's drawing a picture?
Who's playing on the slide?
Who's eating a sandwich?
Who's playing on the swings?

A	woman man girl boy	with	a big hat. a red dress. no hair. long legs. long hair. red shorts. a blue dress.

I like it very much. I don't like it at all.

Who likes meat?

> I like it.

Nadia

> I like it very much.

Bobby

> I quite like it.

Susie

> I don't like it.

Mrs Hill

> I don't like it at all.

Tom

1 Point and ask.

Does she like meat?   Yes, she quite likes it.
Does he like meat?   No, he doesn't like it at all.

2 Ask and answer.

Who likes meat very much?   Bobby.
Who quite likes meat?   Susie.

How much do you like them?

going to a restaurant

watching television

drawing

riding a bicycle

playing football

cooking

swimming

going to the cinema

cleaning my bedroom

going to the dentist

Point and say.

I like cooking. I don't like swimming at all.
I quite like watching television.
I like playing football very much.

Ask your friend.

Do you like going to the cinema?
Do you like cleaning your bedroom?
Do you like swimming?

What can you see on the farm?

farmhouse

tyre

tractor

calf

chicks

lamb

Ask, count and answer.

Mr and Mrs Brown are farmers. This is their farm.
It is spring and there are some baby animals.
The cow has a calf, the hens have some chicks
and the sheep have some lambs.

89

Is anybody there?

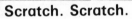

What is he going to do?
What is he doing?
What has he done?

Point and read.

He's going to eat the sandwich.

He's eating it.

He's eaten it.

She's going to put her scarf on.

She's putting it on.

She's put it on.

He's going to draw a picture.

He's drawing it.

He's finished.
He's drawn it.

She's going to drink a bottle of cola.

She's drinking it.

She's finished.
She's drunk it.

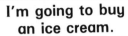

I'm going to buy an ice cream.

I'm buying it.

I've bought it, but I haven't eaten it.

I'm going to school.

I'm at school.

I've been to school. I'm at home now.

We're going to make an omelette.

We're making it.

We've made it!

Be careful! You're going to drop that glass. You're going to break it!

You've dropped it. You've broken it!

Where is it? Where are they?

above

below

behind
back

middle

Mr Martin

Mrs Best

Magda

Alex

left

next to

Karim

right

Susie

Baby

front

Ask and answer.

Who's next to Mrs Best?	Alex.
What's behind Mr Martin?	A tree.
Who's in the middle at the front?	The baby.
Where's the big bird?	It's in the tree. It's above the small bird.

93

Do you like football?

A football game is going to begin.

It has begun!

The football player is going to kick the ball.

He has kicked it!

The football player is going to fall.

He has fallen!

His leg hurts. He says "Ow!!!"

a goalkeeper

At the football game

Now the goat is running away.
A policeman is running after it.

The policeman has fallen.
The goat is coming back.
Is it going to hurt the policeman, too?
No, it's eating his hat!

All the football players
are running after the goat.
It's ten past two now.
That goat has been
on the field since two o'clock.
It's been here for ten minutes.
When will the game begin?

Now the goat's got the ball
and it's running to the fence.
It's going to jump the fence!

Well, the goat has gone,
but the ball has gone, too!
Is there another ball?
Will this football game EVER begin?

Tangrams.

Tangrams are puzzles. They are from China. You begin with a square of paper. You draw lines on it like this, then you cut out the shapes.

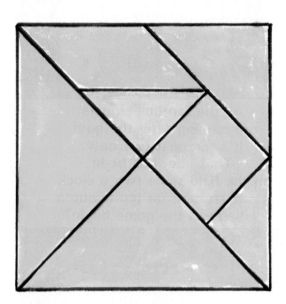

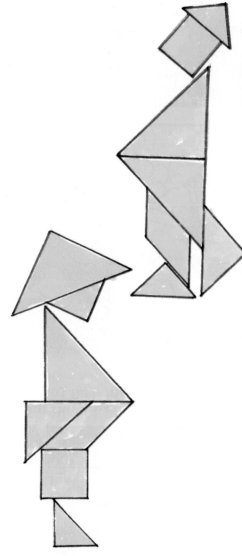

People from China can make thousands of different pictures with these shapes. Here are some of them.

Can you make a tangram puzzle? Use this page to help you. Can you make any other pictures?

Do you like cats? Here is a poem about a cat.

Where, oh where
Has my little cat gone?
Where, oh where
Can it be?
Its ears are short
And its tail is long.
Where, oh where
Can it be?

Where is the cat? Can you see it? What colour is it? What animal is in front of it?

99

PANCAKES

1 Put one cup of flour and a little salt into a bowl.

2 Add an egg to the bowl.

3 Mix a cup of milk slowly into the flour.
Beat for two minutes.
The mixture should be smooth.

4 Put a little butter in a hot pan.
Put a little of the mixture in the pan.

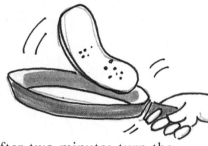

5 After two minutes turn the pancake over.
Cook it for another two minutes.
You should eat the pancake hot with sugar and lemon.

I like pancakes.
I'll make some now.

Alex makes pancakes.

Put flour into a bowl.

Add an egg to the bowl.

Beat for two minutes.

Put a little of the mixture in the pan.

Turn the pancake over.

You should eat the pancake hot with sugar and lemon.

101

Word List

(The words in this list are those which appear for the first time in Level Four.)

The unit number indicates where each word first appears.
* indicates word is spoken only.

word	unit	word	unit
above	11	British	18
ache	12	broken	20
add	16	brushed	9
address	12	bus station	8
Africa	5	butcher	7
after	4	cabbage	7
always	2	calf	22
amazing	6	came	10
American	19	can	3
anorak	2	caretaker	4
anybody	7	carpenter	16
art	8	carrot	3
asked	9	carton	3
asleep	13	cereal	7
attention	11	cheapest	6
Australia	5	chest	12
Australian	5	chicks	22
autumn	2	China	25
baker's	7	chop	7
basement	4	cinema	8
be	4	circles	13
beat	13	circus	6
been	20	clear (the table)	2
before	4	cola	3
begin	15	cold	12
begun	24	college	15
bend down	12	corn flakes	3
best	6	correct	3
biggest	6	cost	3
blindfolded	9	cough	12
block	4	courgettes	7
boots	5	dinosaur	8
both	12	dishes	8
box	3	divide	16
break	15	divided by	16

word	unit	word	unit
dollars	8	geography	15
done	19	get	21
don't	16	got dressed	9
drawn	20	goalkeeper	24
dressed	9	go back	9
drew	17	go forward	9
driver	16	grocer's	7
drop	2	ground	4
drove	17	hare	13
drunk	20	hate	9
earache	12	have	1
easier	8	headache	12
easiest	8	hear	20*
eaten	20	heard	20*
enough	14	hips	12
envelope	17	history	15
ever	2	hole	9
everyone	6	hotel	8
exhibition	8	idea	1
face	12	interesting	8
fallen	24	international	1
far	11	ironed	19
farmer	16	Japanese	19
farmhouse	22	job	16
fastest	13	key	11
fattest	6	kick	24
favourite	15	kicked	24
film star	16	kilo	3
finger	12	kilometre	11
Finland	5	kind	3
finish	12	language	13
Finnish	5	last	11
flag	19	late	9
flat	1	laughed	13
flew	17	least	15
football match	24	let	21
football player	16	letter	16
forward	9	lettuce	7
fridge	3	lift	10
fun	6	light	20

word	unit	word	unit
quite	22	spring	2
race	13	stamp	17
racquet	7	start	15
railway	8	station	8
rainy	5	stomach	12
reach	14	stomach-ache	12
religion	15	story	9
round	3	stripes	19
Russia	19	strongest	6
Russian	19	subject	15
sardines	3	subtract	16
sat	13	Sudan	5
scarf	23	Sudanese	5
science	15	summer	2
scratch	23	sweets	3
season	5	swing	22
secondary school	15	switch on/off	20
seen	20	take out	14
seller	3	tallest	6
send	17	tangram	25
shed	22	tell	11
shortest	6	thinnest	6
shouted	10	thousand	4
shower	9	thumb	12
since	21	tie	20
singer	8	times	16
sink	21	tin	3
sleeves	5	tired	19
slide	22	toothache	12
smart	20	top	4
smooth	25	tortoise	13
soap powder	3	touch	9
somebody	9	touched	10
something	9	towards	13
sometimes	2	tractor	22
soon	13	tyre	22
Spain	19	understand	13
Spanish	19	United States	19
speaking	13	usually	2
spinach	7	vegetable	7